W9-BCJ-871

TABLE OF CONTENTS

Fetch!

CHIHUAHUAS

Valerie Bodden

Creative Education · Creative Paperbacks

published by Creative Education and Creative Paperbacks
P.O. Box 227, Mankato, Minnesota 56002
Creative Education and Creative Paperbacks are imprints of
The Creative Company
www.thecreativecompany.us

design and production by Christine Vanderbeek
art direction by Rita Marshall
printed in the United States of America

photographs by Alamy (AF archive), Getty Images (Vern
Evans Photo), iStockphoto (baratroli, fstop123, GlobalP,
onetouchspark, rusm, utkamandarinka), Shutterstock
(Utekhina Anna, Grisha Bruev, Cressida studio, cyno-
club, Pavel Hlystov, Eric Isselee, Jagodka, kamilpetran,
Matej Kastelic, MirasWonderland, Neveshkin Nikolay,
Scorpp, SCOTTCHAN, Viorel Sima, SmileStudio, Andrey
Starostin, steamroller_blues, Vitaly Titov, Nikolai Tsvetkov,
WilleeCole Photography, Jeerasak Wongkittithon)

copyright © 2018 creative education, creative paperbacks
International copyright reserved in all countries. No part of
this book may be reproduced in any form without written
permission from the publisher.

library of congress cataloging-in-publication data
Names: Bodden, Valerie, author.
Title: Chihuahuas / Valerie Bodden.
Series: Fetch!
Includes bibliographical references and index.
Summary: A brief overview of the physical characteristics,
personality traits, and habits of the Chihuahua breed, as
well as descriptions of famous pop-culture Chihuahuas
such as Gidget.
Identifiers:
ISBN 978-1-60818-898-7 (hardcover)
ISBN 978-1-62832-514-0 (pbk)
ISBN 978-1-56660-950-0 (eBook)
This title has been submitted for CIP processing under
LCCN 2017938923.
CCSS: RI.1.1, 2, 4, 5, 6, 7; RI.2.1, 2, 5, 6, 7;
RI.3.1, 5, 7; RF.1.1, 3, 4; RF.2.3, 4

first edition HC 9 8 7 6 5 4 3 2 1
first edition PBK 9 8 7 6 5 4 3 2 1

TINY CHIHUAHUAS

A Chihuahua is a *breed* of dog. Chihuahuas are the smallest dogs in the world. But they like to have big fun! Chihuahuas are smart and playful. They like to please their owners.

WHAT DO CHIHUAHUAS LOOK LIKE?

Chihuahuas have small, rounded heads. They have big eyes. Their ears are *erect*. A Chihuahua's pointy tail can curl up over its back.

Most Chihuahuas have dark brown eyes.

Most Chihuahuas are only six to nine inches (15.2–22.9 cm) tall. They weigh about six pounds (2.7 kg). That's about the weight of a newborn baby. Chihuahuas can have short or long fur. The fur can be black, brown, gray, red, tan, or white. Or it can be more than one color.

CHIHUAHUA PUPPIES

A newborn Chihuahua puppy weighs less than half a pound (0.2 kg). But the puppies grow quickly. They have floppy ears at first. The ears stand up straighter as the puppies grow.

Chihuahuas are almost fully grown by six months of age.

CHIHUAHUAS IN THE MOVIES

Chihuahuas have been in many movies. A whole *cast* of Chihuahuas starred in the 2008 movie *Beverly Hills Chihuahua*. Tito is a cartoon Chihuahua in the Walt Disney movie *Oliver and Company* (1988). In the 2001 movie *Legally Blonde*, a Chihuahua named Bruiser goes everywhere with his owner.

Bruiser (left) is owned by Elle Woods.

CHIHUAHUAS AND PEOPLE

Chihuahuas most likely came from Mexico. They are the oldest breed of dogs in the Americas. Today, many Chihuahuas work as *therapy dogs*.

Chihuahuas enjoy spending time with their owners.

Chihuahuas are popular pets. Chihuahua puppies are cute. But they can be a lot of work. Some are scared by loud children. Because they are so small, puppies are easily hurt, too. Adult Chihuahuas can be easier to care for.

Tiny Chihuahuas are good apartment dogs.

WHAT DO CHIHUAHUAS LIKE TO DO?

Chihuahuas need to live indoors. They can get their exercise by running around their home. They love to follow their owners around. Some Chihuahuas will curl up on their owner's lap, too!

Chihuahuas must be covered or clothed in cold weather.

Chihuahuas love to learn new tricks. Turn on some music and teach your Chihuahua to dance. You will both have lots of fun!

A FAMOUS CHIHUAHUA

Gidget was a Chihuahua who starred in
Taco Bell **commercials** (*cuh-MUR-shulz*).
She was supposed to play a small part.
But then she became the star! That meant
Gidget had to play the part of a boy dog.
In 2003, Gidget played Bruiser's mom in
the movie *Legally Blonde 2*. She had a
role in *Beverly Hills Chihuahua*, too.

GLOSSARY

breed a kind of an animal with certain traits, such as long ears or a good nose

cast the actors in a movie, play, or TV show

commercials short ads meant to make people want to buy a product

erect standing upright

therapy dogs dogs that help people who are sick or hurt by letting the people pet and enjoy them

READ MORE

Green, Sara. *Chihuahuas*. Minneapolis: Bellwether Media, 2010.

Heos, Bridget. *Do You Really Want a Dog?* North Mankato, Minn.: Amicus, 2014.

Johnson, Jinny. *Puppy*. North Mankato, Minn.: Smart Apple Media, 2014.

WEBSITES

American Kennel Club: Chihuahua
http://www.akc.org/dog-breeds/chihuahua/
Learn more about Chihuahuas, and check out lots of Chihuahua pictures.

Bailey's Responsible Dog Owner's Coloring Book
http://classic.akc.org/pdfs/public_education/coloring_book.pdf
Print out pictures to color, and learn more about caring for a pet dog.

Every effort has been made to ensure that these sites are suitable for children, that they have educational value, and that they contain no inappropriate material. However, because of the nature of the Internet, it is impossible to guarantee that these sites will remain active indefinitely or that their contents will not be altered.

INDEX